Your Pregnancy *Journal*

Your Pregnancy *Journal*

Glade B. Curtis, M.D., F.A.C.O.G.
and
Judith Schuler, M.S.

PERSEUS PUBLISHING
Cambridge, Massachusetts

Many of the designations used by manufacturers and sellers to distinguish their products are claimed as trademarks. Where those designations appear in this book and Perseus Publishing was aware of a trademark claim, the designations have been printed in initial capital letters.

Cataloging-in-Publication Data is available from the Library of Congress
ISBN 0–55561-343-8

Perseus Publishing is a member of the Perseus Books Group.
Find us on the World Wide Web at http://www.perseuspublishing.com

Perseus Publishing books are available at special discounts for bulk purchases in the U.S. by corporations, institutions, and other organizations. For more information, please contact the Special Markets Department at the Perseus Books Group, 11 Cambridge Center, Cambridge, MA 02142, or call (800) 255-1514 or (617) 252-5298, or e-mail j.mccrary@perseusbooks.com.

Illustrations by Les Young
Text design by Trish Wilkinson
Set in 12-point Simoncini Garamond by the Perseus Books Group

First printing, March 2002

2 3 4 5 6 7 8 9 10—05 04 03

Contents

This diary/journal belongs to:

In anticipation of the birth of:

Due on:

Born on:

Baby's weight:

Baby's height:

Hospital where born:

Those in attendance:

Important Telephone Numbers

Doctor

Hospital

Partner's office/work

Partner's pager or cellular phone number

Family members/close friends

Other important numbers

Ambulance

Fire

Police/Sheriff

Poison control

My *Firsts* during This Pregnancy

First thought I might be pregnant

*First learned I **was** pregnant*

First told my partner I was pregnant

First told family members and friends I was pregnant

First doctor's visit

First heard baby's heartbeat

First ultrasound

First felt baby move

First education/prenatal class

Partner first felt baby move

Other firsts

Special thoughts

Weeks 1 & 2

Week beginning Sunday _____

You probably don't know you are pregnant at this time, but after you learn you are, you may want to go back and fill in your thoughts and feelings for this week.

The Baby's Due Date— It Helps to Have a Goal

*A*n important consideration in any pregnancy is figuring out when your baby is due. You probably don't know the date your baby was conceived, but you probably know the date of your last menstrual period. Your doctor will use this date as the starting point of your pregnancy to help him or her decide when to do tests and to help measure the growth of your baby.

A pregnancy typically lasts about 280 days (40 weeks) from the *first day of bleeding* of your last menstrual period. To get an approximate delivery date, count back 3 months from the first day of your last period, and add 7 days.

Pregnancy time is usually counted in weeks. These weeks are divided into three time periods, called *trimesters,* each about 13 weeks long. You'll probably hear other definitions of pregnancy time, including gestational age, ovulatory age and lunar months. *Gestational age* begins from the first day of your

1

Finding out you're pregnant is the beginning of an exciting adventure for you and your partner.

last menstrual period. This is the most-used reference to discuss pregnancy. *Ovulatory age* begins on the day you conceive. This is the actual age of your developing baby. *Lunar months* refers to a 28-day period; a pregnancy lasts 10 lunar months.

You might find these different references a bit confusing, but it's important to know about them. When you have a discussion with your doctor, it helps to know what he or she is talking about.

Think of your due date as a date to look forward to and to prepare for. Only 5% of all babies are actually born on their due date.

How big is my baby?

What changes are occurring in my baby?

How big am I?

How am I feeling?

How is my partner feeling?

Questions for my doctor

Things to do this week

Special thoughts and feelings about this week

A Place for Special Remembrances

Use this space for keeping
special mementoes in your journal.

Week 3

You probably don't know you are pregnant this week, but after you learn you are, you may want to go back and fill in your thoughts and feelings for this week.

"I Can't Wait— I Have to Know for Sure" *(Are You Really Pregnant?)*

*I*t's exciting to think you might be expecting a baby. When you suspect you might be, one of the first things you may want to do is take a home pregnancy test. Before you buy a home pregnancy test or call your doctor's office about having a pregnancy test, look for the signs and symptoms of pregnancy. If you experience them, the next step is a pregnancy test.

Signs and Symptoms of Pregnancy

- Missed menstrual period
- Nausea with or without vomiting
- Fatigue
- Breast changes and breast tenderness
- Frequent urination

If you really can't wait to take the test, use a home pregnancy test, available at the drugstore. There are many tests on the market, and they are very reliable if you use them correctly. Most are very easy to use, and some are almost error-proof. If the test is positive, contact your doctor to make your first prenatal appointment.

If you call your doctor, believing you might be pregnant, you may be asked to do a home pregnancy test to help determine if you are pregnant *before* you go to the office. Home tests are so accurate now that some doctors rely on them as an initial screening for pregnancy. Sometimes a woman misses a period because of stress, excessive physical exertion or dieting, and she is not pregnant. If your test is positive, an appointment will be made for you to see the doctor.

In the past, tests that could predict a pregnancy very early were only available through your doctor's office. Today, home pregnancy tests have become increasingly sensitive and can show positive results even before you miss a menstrual period. Most tests are positive 7 to 10 days after you conceive! Most doctors recommend you wait until you miss your period before having a test to save you money and emotional energy.

How big is my baby?

What changes are occurring in my baby?

How big am I?

How am I feeling?

How is my partner feeling?

Questions for my doctor

Things to do this week

Special thoughts and feelings about this week

A Place for Special Remembrances

Use this space for keeping special mementoes in your journal.

Week 4

Week beginning Sunday _____

You probably don't know you are pregnant this week, but after you learn you are, you may want to go back and fill in your thoughts and feelings for this week.

Keep All Your Prenatal Appointments

If you are pregnant, one of the most important things you can do for yourself and your developing baby is to get good prenatal care for your entire pregnancy.

What is prenatal care? It is the special care from healthcare professionals that you receive during pregnancy. It is designed to help you have a healthy pregnancy and to identify any pregnancy problems or conditions before they become serious.

If you have confidence in your doctor and his or her healthcare team, you'll be able to relax and to enjoy your pregnancy. Pregnancy is a special time in your life; good prenatal care helps ensure you do everything possible to make it the best 9 months possible for your growing baby, too.

Your first prenatal visit may be one of the longest. Your doctor will ask questions, order lab tests and give you a physical

Prenatal care is important for your good health and the health of your developing baby. Keep all appointments, take any medications prescribed for you and undergo any tests your physician recommends.

examination. This is done to establish a baseline of your health as you enter your pregnancy.

When a complete medical history is taken, your doctor asks about your menstrual periods, recent birth-control methods, previous pregnancies and other details. If you have a chronic medical condition, discuss it at this first visit. Tell your doctor about any medications you take or those you are allergic to. Be sure to have a list of *all* substances you take—over-the-counter and prescription medications, vitamins, herbs and botanicals. Be sure you know the dose or amount you take each day. Include the amount of caffeine you consume, too, if you use caffeinated products.

Your family's past medical history may be important, such as a history of diabetes or high blood pressure. If you have medical records, bring them; they are important.

On your first visit, you'll probably have a pelvic exam. It helps determine if your uterus is the appropriate size for how far along you are in your pregnancy. A Pap smear is done if you haven't had one in the last year, and other tests may be required.

> Always feel free to ask questions about your pregnancy at your prenatal checkups.

In most cases, you'll visit your doctor every 4 weeks for the first 7 months, then every 2 weeks until the last month, then once a week. In this journal, we have provided pages to record information on each of your prenatal visits. See page 180. You may want to take this journal with you when you go to office visits so you can write in information as you receive it.

You may be scheduled for visits more frequently, if your doctor believes they are necessary. On every visit, your weight and blood pressure will be checked; they provide valuable information about how your pregnancy is progressing. Later in pregnancy, your abdomen will also be measured.

Be sure you keep all your prenatal appointments. Your doctor can follow your progress and your baby's development more easily if he or she sees you on a regular basis. In that way, problems can be addressed early and resolved as quickly as possible.

> Record information you receive at your prenatal visits on the pages provided for this purpose, which begin on page 180.

How big is my baby?

What changes are occurring in my baby?

How big am I?

How am I feeling?

How is my partner feeling?

Questions for my doctor

Things to do this week

Special thoughts and feelings about this week

Week 5

Week beginning Sunday _____

You probably don't know you are pregnant this week, but after you learn you are, you may want to go back and fill in your thoughts and feelings for this week.

Morning Sickness—Even if It Lasts All Day Long!

An early symptom of pregnancy you may (or may not) experience is nausea, sometimes accompanied by vomiting. It is often called *morning sickness.*

Morning sickness is typically present at the beginning of pregnancy and is usually worse in the morning (it often improves during the day). But we know of some women who experience it at night or all through the day, so if you have it at any time of the day during your pregnancy, it *is* morning sickness!

Morning sickness usually begins around week 6 and lasts until week 12 or 13, when it starts to subside. For some woman, it can last throughout their entire pregnancy.

A pill to help relieve the symptoms of morning sickness is available and is called *Bendectin.* It can prevent or decrease the symptoms of nausea during pregnancy. You might want to ask your doctor about it.

If morning sickness causes you to be absent from your job, it's important for you to know about the Family Medical Leave Act (FMLA), passed in 1993. This law states you do *not* need a doctor's note to give to an employer verifying the problem of morning sickness during pregnancy. Nausea and vomiting from pregnancy is classified as a "chronic condition" and may require you to be out occasionally, but you don't need a doctor's treatment.

There are ways you can deal with the nausea and vomiting you may experience. Try the suggestions in the box on the opposite page to help you feel better. And take heart—your discomfort should pass fairly soon, and you'll be feeling better again.

Ways to Deal with Morning Sickness

If you suffer from nausea or vomiting during pregnancy, try the suggestions below to help you feel better.

• Eat small portions of food your stomach can handle throughout the day, instead of three large meals.
• Eat a snack, such as dry crackers or rice cakes, *before* you get out of bed in the morning. Or ask your partner to make you some dry toast.
• Avoid heavy, fatty foods.
• Keep up your fluid intake—fluids may be easier to handle than solids and will help you avoid dehydration.
• Take it easy when you feel nauseated. Sitting down and relaxing may help you feel better.
• If you find some foods that help you deal with your nausea, even if they aren't on the recommended list, eat them. One woman was nauseated by toast, but pickled herring calmed her stomach!
• Alternate wet foods with dry foods. Eat only dry foods at one meal, then wet foods or liquids at the next.
• Try fresh ginger—it's a natural remedy for nausea. Grate it onto vegetables and other foods.
• Avoid things that trigger your nausea, such as odors, movement or noise.
• Suck on a fresh-cut lemon when you feel nauseous.
• Get lots of rest.
• Avoid getting overheated, which can contribute to your nausea.
• If you do vomit, brush your teeth or rinse your mouth out as soon as you can.

How big is my baby?

What changes are occurring in my baby?

How big am I?

How am I feeling?

How is my partner feeling?

Questions for my doctor

Things to do this week

Special thoughts and feelings about this week

Week 6

You probably don't know you are pregnant this week, but after you learn you are, you may want to go back and fill in your thoughts and feelings for this week.

It's Hard Work
Being a Mother-to-Be

*D*uring the first part of your pregnancy, you may be exhausted! It may be difficult to get up in the morning, or you may feel like going to bed at 8:00 P.M. One of the most important things on your mind may be getting enough rest.

Fatigue is one of the first signs of pregnancy. It's also one that often gets better as your pregnancy progresses. Do yourself a favor, and rest or take it easy whenever you can.

Don't lie on your back or stomach when you sleep or rest, even this early in pregnancy. It may not seem important now, but as your uterus gets larger, it presses on blood vessels that run down the back of your abdomen. When you lie on your back, you decrease circulation to the lower parts of your body *and* to your baby. It may also be harder to breathe when you lie on your back. Learn to sleep on your side early in pregnancy; you'll be glad you did as you get bigger. Many women find

17

Now that you're pregnant, you may feel more tired than you ever have before! Try to rest whenever you can. A good night's sleep can help you feel much better.

"pregnancy pillows" that support the entire body offer great relief.

When you are resting and relaxing, elevate your feet to keep blood moving throughout your body, especially your legs. Rest your legs on a pillow. Watch your diet, and drink lots of fluids. Avoid sugar because it can make fatigue worse. Start now to learn to sleep on your side.

If you can't sleep enough at night to make you feel rested, nap during the day. If you can't nap, sit down and relax—listen to music or read, if that helps. When you relax, prop your feet above your chest or lie on your side to help ease any swelling or discomfort in your legs.

Tips for Getting a Good Night's Sleep

Try these suggestions if you find you are not getting enough rest at night.

- Go to bed and wake up the same time each day.
- Don't drink too much fluid at night. Decrease fluid intake after 6:00 P.M. so you won't have to get up to go to the bathroom all night long.
- Avoid caffeine after late afternoon.
- Don't eat heavy meals at night; they may cause indigestion.
- If you eat snacks in the evening, don't eat foods that disagree with you or that may cause you problems later.
- A soothing, warm (not hot) bath at night may help you relax enough to go to sleep easily.
- Get regular exercise.
- Sleep in a cool bedroom—70F (21.2C) is about the highest temperature comfortable for sleeping.
- If you experience heartburn at night, sleep propped up.

How big is my baby?

What changes are occurring in my baby?

How big am I?

How am I feeling?

How is my partner feeling?

Questions for my doctor

Things to do this week

Special thoughts and feelings about this week

Week 7

Week beginning Sunday _____

You may not know you are pregnant this week, but after you learn you are, you may want to go back and fill in your thoughts and feelings for this week.

You're Working Out for Two— Exercising during Pregnancy

*I*s it safe to exercise during pregnancy? Experts agree exercise during pregnancy is OK for most pregnant women, if it is done properly. To be on the safe side, discuss exercising with your doctor at your first prenatal visit. If you decide later to start exercising or to change your current exercise program, be sure to talk with your physician *before* you begin or make any changes.

Many women exercise regularly before pregnancy and want to continue while they are pregnant. Exercise helps them feel fit, control their weight and look their best. If you exercised on a regular basis before you became pregnant, talk to your doctor about continuing during this time. You may need to modify your exercise goals and take things easier during pregnancy.

Changes in your body may require changes in your exercise routine. Your center of gravity shifts, so you may need to adjust

21

your exercise for that change. As your abdomen grows larger, you may not be able to do some activities very comfortably, and you may have to eliminate others.

During pregnancy, your heart rate is higher; you don't have to exercise as vigorously to reach your target-heart-rate range. If your heart rate is too high, slow down but don't stop completely. Continue exercising at a moderate rate. If your heart rate is too low and you don't feel winded, you may pick up the pace a bit, but don't overdo it. Check your pulse rate frequently to make sure you aren't overexerting.

When you exercise, drink a cup of water before you begin your routine. Then drink ½ cup to 1 cup of water every 20 minutes while you exercise to help prevent dehydration.

Some women don't like to exercise or don't exercise on a regular basis. When they discover they're pregnant, they begin to think about the benefits of exercise. They want to know whether it is safe to begin an exercise program during pregnancy. If you've never exercised before, you *must* discuss it with your doctor before you begin.

If your pregnancy is uncomplicated, you should be able to exercise as long as you feel comfortable. Don't do too much, too fast. Most moderate exercise is safe.

Begin with *moderate* exercise if you don't have a regular exercise routine. Walking is an excellent choice. Riding a stationary bike can be enjoyable. Swimming and other water exercises are also good for a beginner; the water provides your body with a lot of support.

A Water Workout

- Pool water should be warm but not hot. The ideal temperature of pool water is between 80 and 84F (26.5 and 29C).

- Avoid hot tubs and spas because the water is too hot for the fetus.

- Drink plenty of fluid before you begin exercising and during exercise. Dehydration can occur even in a pool.

- If you work out in an outdoor pool, wear water-proof sunscreen.

- While walking on a pool deck, watch your step. It's easy to slip and fall around water.

- Take care of your skin when you get out of the water by using moisturizing lotions.

- Eat easily digested foods ½ to 1 hour before you work out; choose fruit or whole-wheat products.

- To help you keep your footing when you exercise in the pool, wear aquatic shoes, tennis shoes or jogging shoes. Be sure the shoe you choose has a good tread so you don't slip.

- Exercise with hand paddles or flippers to increase water resistance.

- Take it easy—even if it doesn't feel like you're working very hard, it is possible to work out too hard in any exercise setting.

How big is my baby?

What changes are occurring in my baby?

How big am I?

How am I feeling?

How is my partner feeling?

Questions for my doctor

Things to do this week

Special thoughts and feelings about this week

Week 8

You may not know you are pregnant this week, but after you learn you are, you may want to go back and fill in your thoughts and feelings for this week.

Changes in Your Breasts

Breast changes during pregnancy are common. Nearly every woman experiences some sort of change. A woman's breasts contain connective tissue for support, fatty tissue for protection and milk-producing glands for feeding a baby. The breast actually produces *more* milk glands during pregnancy, as it readies to provide nourishment for baby.

At about 8 weeks, your breasts will probably begin to get larger; you may notice they are lumpy or nodular. They may feel tender or sore, or they may tingle during pregnancy.

Your breasts may change color slightly. Before pregnancy, the areola (the area that surrounds the nipple) is usually pink. During pregnancy, it is common for it to turn brown or red-brown. It may also grow larger during pregnancy and lactation. Some researchers believe these changes occur as a signal to the breastfeeding infant.

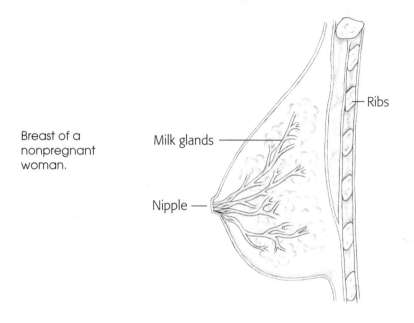

Breast of a
nonpregnant
woman.

Milk glands

Nipple

Ribs

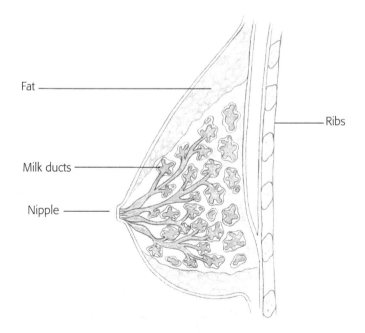

Fat

Milk ducts

Nipple

Ribs

Breast of a pregnant woman. Notice the increase in the number of milk glands in the breast in preparation for feeding baby.

During the second trimester, breasts form a thin yellow fluid called *colostrum*. It is the precursor to breast milk. Sometimes it may leak from your breasts, or it can be expressed by squeezing the nipples (but it's a good idea *not* to do this).

Some women's nipples are *inverted;* they are flat or retract (invert) into the breast. If you have inverted nipples, you may find it more difficult to breastfeed, but breastfeeding isn't impossible. To see if you have inverted nipples, place your thumb and index finger on the areola. Gently compress the base of the nipple; if it flattens or retracts into the breast, you have inverted nipples. Plastic breast shields worn under your bra during the last few weeks of pregnancy create a slight pressure at the base of the nipple that helps draw out the nipple. Ask your doctor for further information.

The average woman's breast weighs about 6 to 7 ounces before pregnancy. By the end of pregnancy, each breast may weigh between 14 and 28 ounces! Because breasts grow larger during pregnancy, it's important to buy and to wear a good bra that fits well. Maternity bras are made especially for this purpose. Whatever type of bra you wear (it's a good idea to wear a bra during pregnancy, even if you don't usually wear one), be sure it is comfortable, offers you support and provides you room to grow!

How big is my baby?

What changes are occurring in my baby?

How big am I?

How am I feeling?

How is my partner feeling?

Questions for my doctor

Things to do this week

Special thoughts and feelings about this week

Week 9

Week beginning Sunday _____

You may not know you are pregnant this week, but after you learn you are, you may want to go back and fill in your thoughts and feelings for this week.

"Why Do I Have to Have so Many Tests?"

*M*edical tests are important in your prenatal care. Every test provides your doctor with information; this information is used to plan the best course of treatment for you and your growing baby. The test most pregnant couples want to know about is ultrasound. It is discussed in Week 18.

Your doctor will probably order a lot of tests during your first or second prenatal visit. See the box on the following page for a list of some tests you may have. Results of these tests give your doctor information so he or she can provide the best care for you. Later in pregnancy, your doctor may repeat some tests or order new tests. For example, the 28th week of pregnancy is the best time to pick up blood-sugar problems.

In addition to those tests listed on the next page, you will be weighed and your blood pressure checked at every prenatal visit. These two tests provide a great deal of information. Not gaining enough weight, or gaining too much, can indicate problems. Changes in blood-pressure readings alert your doctor to potential problems. After about 20 weeks, your abdomen will also be measured at every visit; see the discussion in Week 10. Your doctor will also listen to the fetal heartbeat.

Feel free to ask about any test your doctor recommends— why it is done, what the results will show and how the results can help you and your baby. This is important information.

Tests Your Doctor May Order

The tests listed below may be ordered at your first or second prenatal visit:

- a complete blood count (CBC) to check iron stores and to check for infections
- urinalysis and urine culture
- a test for syphilis
- cervical cultures, as indicated
- rubella titers, for immunity against rubella
- blood type
- Rh-factor
- a test for hepatitis-B antibodies
- alpha-fetoprotein
- triple screen
- Pap smear

How big is my baby?

What changes are occurring in my baby?

How big am I?

How am I feeling?

How is my partner feeling?

Questions for my doctor

Things to do this week

Special thoughts and feelings about this week

A Place for Special Remembrances

Use this space for keeping
special mementoes in your journal.

Week 10

Measuring Baby's Growth

When you go to your prenatal visits, you may be surprised when the doctor pulls out a tape measure to measure your tummy. No, it's not to see how big your waist is getting! Your doctor uses a tape measure to determine how much your uterus is growing and how your baby is developing.

Different doctors measure a woman's abdominal growth differently. Some measure from the bellybutton. Others measure from the pubic symphysis, which is the bony midpoint in the pelvic bone. (When you aren't pregnant, this bony area is 6 to 10 inches below your bellybutton, depending on how tall you are.)

Measurement begins after about 20 weeks because your uterus is getting big enough to see the changes in it. From that point, you should grow about 0.4 inch (1cm) each week.

You may be wondering why this measurement is important. It's a routine test you have when you go to the doctor, much like taking your blood pressure or weighing you. It gives your doctor insight as to how your pregnancy is growing and progressing. A measurement that seems too small from one office visit to the next might mean your due date is incorrect. A measurement that seems too big may indicate twins! Your doctor will order further tests or treatment, if he or she believes there is reason for doing so.

If you are seen by a doctor you don't normally see, your measurements may be a bit different than they normally would be. It doesn't mean there is a problem or that someone measured you incorrectly. Everyone measures a little differently.

Don't compare your measurement with other pregnant women's measurements. They are different for different women. They may also be different for the same woman from one pregnancy to another!

How big is my baby?

What changes are occurring in my baby?

How big am I?

How am I feeling?

How is my partner feeling?

Questions for my doctor

Things to do this week

Special thoughts and feelings about this week

A Place for Special Remembrances

Use this space for keeping
special mementoes in your journal.

Week 11

"Can I Eat Anything I Want Now?"

*I*t's a fact—if you eat healthfully during pregnancy, you're more likely to have a healthy baby. Your good nutrition meets the nutritional needs of the baby growing inside you. The quality of your calories is very important.

Eat healthfully during your pregnancy. Choose foods that provide nutrition and meet the needs of you and your growing baby.

Have you heard the saying, "a pregnant woman is eating for two"? Some women believe this means they can eat twice as much as they normally do. Not true! What it really means is that you must get the best nutrition for both you and your growing baby.

If your weight is in the normal range before pregnancy, your caloric intake should average about 2200 calories a day during the first trimester of pregnancy. You need to add up to 300 calories to that number for the remainder of your pregnancy, depending on your prepregnancy weight.

Why the extra calories? They are needed to help deal with the tissue growth in you and your baby. Your baby uses the calories to create and to store protein, fat and carbohydrates, and to provide energy for its bodily processes. Extra calories also support the changes in your body; your uterus increases in size many times, your breast size increases and your blood volume increases by 50%, among other changes.

Choose foods carefully. You can't eat just anything and expect to get the best nutrition for you and your growing baby; eating right takes care and attention. Eat foods high in vitamins and minerals, especially iron, calcium, magnesium, folic acid and zinc. Fiber and fluids are necessary to help with constipation problems associated with pregnancy. Eating a variety of healthy foods each day supplies you with the nutrients you need. Choose from dairy products, protein foods, fruits and vegetables, and breads and cereals.

Avoid junk food and foods loaded with empty calories. They can add extra weight, and they provide little nutrition.

Where your calories come from is as important as the number you consume. A good rule of thumb to follow is: if a food grows in the ground or on trees, it's better for you that if it comes from a can or a box.

How big is my baby?

What changes are occurring in my baby?

How big am I?

How am I feeling?

How is my partner feeling?

Questions for my doctor

Things to do this week

Special thoughts and feelings about this week

$\mathcal{A}$ $\mathcal{P}lace$ for $\mathcal{S}pecial$ $\mathcal{R}emembrances$

Use this space for keeping
special mementoes in your journal.

Week 12

Hearing Your Baby's Heartbeat— This Is the Good Part

*S*omething you'll be looking forward to is hearing your baby's heartbeat. Many women have said that when they hear their baby's heart beating, the fact they have a life growing inside them becomes very real.

A special listening machine, called a *doppler,* magnifies the sound of the baby's heartbeat so it can be heard. It may be possible to hear the baby's heartbeat around your 12-week visit. If your doctor doesn't offer it to you, ask about it. If doppler equipment is not available, it may be possible to hear the heartbeat around 20 weeks with a stethoscope. The ability to hear the heartbeat with a stethoscope usually occurs after a woman feels her baby move.

The baby's heartbeat sounds like a swishing sound when you listen to it. Your heartbeat, which you may also hear, is a definite beating sound. Your heart rate is about 60 to 80 beats a minute; your baby's will be much faster—about 120 to 160 beats a minute.

Hearing your baby's heartbeat is exciting for you and your partner. The first time you hear the heartbeat is a good visit to ask your partner to go to with you. Once you've heard it, you may want to brings others—it's exciting for them, too. If you'd like to take your mother or mother-in-law to an office visit for the experience, ask at the doctor's office if it's OK. Older children might also enjoy hearing baby's heartbeat. Clear them with office staff *before* your bring them with you.

How big is my baby?

What changes are occurring in my baby?

How big am I?

How am I feeling?

How is my partner feeling?

Questions for my doctor

Things to do this week

Special thoughts and feelings about this week

A Place for Special Remembrances

Use this space for keeping
special mementoes in your journal.

Week 13

Week beginning Sunday _____

Start Managing
Your Weight *Now*

As hard as it may be for you, you *need* to gain a certain amount of weight during your pregnancy. When you gain the correct amount of weight, it helps ensure that you and your baby are healthy at the time of delivery.

In the past, weight gain for pregnant women was very restricted. Thirty years ago, some women were allowed to gain only 15 pounds! Today, pregnancy recommendations for weight gain are higher; normal weight gain is 25 to 35 pounds. If you are underweight when you begin pregnancy, expect to gain between 28 and 40 pounds. If you're overweight, you probably shouldn't gain as much weight as other women during pregnancy. Acceptable weight gain for you may be between 15 and 25 pounds. Recommendations vary; your doctor will decide what's right for you.

You may look at 25 to 35 pounds as a lot of weight to gain. Spread over your entire pregnancy, it's about ⅔ of a pound (10 ounces) a week until 20 weeks, then 1 pound a week through the 40th week. It's important to pay attention to your weight gain.

If you have morning sickness at the beginning of your pregnancy or if you're overly fatigued, you may not gain weight, or

Getting weighed every time you go to the doctor's office is one way
your healthcare team watches over your developing pregnancy.

you may even lose a little weight early in pregnancy. Your doctor will keep track of weight changes.

Don't be obsessive about your weight. If you're in good
shape when you get pregnant, with an appropriate amount of
body fat, and you exercise regularly and eat healthfully during
your pregnancy, you shouldn't have a problem with excessive
weight gain.

Where Does the Weight Go?	
7½ pounds	baby
7 pounds	maternal stores
2 pounds	breasts
2 pounds	uterus
2 pounds	amniotic fluid
4 pounds	increased fluid volume
1½ pounds	placenta

How big is my baby?

What changes are occurring in my baby?

How big am I?

How am I feeling?

How is my partner feeling?

Questions for my doctor

Things to do this week

Special thoughts and feelings about this week

A Place for Special Remembrances

Use this space for keeping special mementoes in your journal.

Week 14

Benefits of Pregnancy— There *Are* Some Advantages

*D*id you know that being pregnant can be beneficial for you? Recent research has shown that pregnancy can actually help a woman in various ways. Some of these benefits can last for many years!

If you suffer from allergies or asthma, you may feel better during pregnancy. While you're pregnant, your body produces natural steroids. These steroids can help reduce allergy and asthma symptoms.

Pregnancy may protect you from breast cancer and ovarian cancer later in life. The younger you are when you begin having babies, and the more pregnancies you have, the greater the benefits.

If you suffer from migraine headaches, you may find some relief during pregnancy. Migraine headaches often disappear during the second and third trimesters.

Because you won't be having periods while you're pregnant, menstrual cramps are a thing of the past. And great news—after pregnancy, they may not return!

Along these same lines, pregnancy stops growth of endometrial tissue when ovulation stops. If you suffer from moderate endometriosis, pregnancy may help.

If you have rheumatoid arthritis, systemic lupus erythematosus, inflammatory bowel disease or any other autoimmune disorder, you may feel better during pregnancy. The natural steroids produced by the placenta that affect allergies and asthma may also affect inflammation, which is common in these diseases.

Announcing Your Pregnancy to Family and Friends

Is it time to announce your pregnancy to family and friends? You may already have told your parents or a close friend. Have you thought about who you will tell and how you will make the announcement?

We often recommend not telling anyone your exciting news until you have heard the baby's heartbeat, at about 12 weeks. At this point, the chance of miscarriage is low. But it can be hard to wait that long.

There are a lot of cute, clever ways to make your announcement. T-shirts stating, "I'm going to be a Mom" or "I'm going to be a parent" are available. If you have another child or children, a T-shirt with "I'm going to be a big sister" or "I'm going to be a big brother" is a fun way to spread the news. You might want to have a special dinner for family members and serve a cake with the news written on it.

Don't despair if you don't announce your news with a cake or T-shirts. Sometimes it's just too exciting, and you just blurt out the news!

How big is my baby?

What changes are occurring in my baby?

How big am I?

How am I feeling?

How is my partner feeling?

Questions for my doctor

Things to do this week

Special thoughts and feelings about this week

A Place for Special Remembrances

Use this space for keeping
special mementoes in your journal.

Week 15

Week beginning Sunday _____

Is It a Girl?
Is It a Boy?

*J*ust about every parent wonders if their baby is a girl or a boy. When your baby is born, your doctor will be able to tell you definitely what sex the baby is. Before that, you have a 50–50 chance of guessing correctly!

"What is my baby's sex?" is one of the most frequently asked questions—and not just of healthcare professionals! For years, women have attempted to determine the sex of their baby by doing some pretty unusual things. For hundreds of years, it was the "wedding ring on a string" test. When we were having our children, it was the "Drano test." An old wives' tale said dreaming about the baby's sex was a sure way to know what it was. Others said the heartbeat of the baby could indicate its sex—a fast heart rate indicated a girl and a slower heart rate indicated a boy. Some say the way a woman carries the baby reveals its sex—a boy is carried all out in front, and a girl is carried more around the sides.

We're lucky today. We *do* have tests that can determine the baby's sex. Some of the tests are almost routine now, such as ultrasound. With the advances in the ultrasound test itself, and the increased experience and knowledge of those who perform the test, a prediction of a baby's sex is much more reliable.

Amniocentesis is a sure way to predict the sex of a baby; however, the test is not done for this reason unless there is a medical reason to know a baby's sex before it is born. One example is to predict hemophilia so precautions may be taken to care for the baby soon after birth.

You probably want to know your baby's sex, but it's kind of fun when you don't, too. You can dream about doing special things with your little girl or little boy. You can consider names for girls and boys. You can anticipate the arrival of your baby without knowing whether you will welcome a daughter or a son. You can look forward to your life with this person you have not yet met.

Baby Names

It's not too early to start thinking about names for your baby. You might want to get a baby-name book, or ask family members about family names you might not know about. Write down names for girls and for boys, then think about them for a while. Add or delete names as your pregnancy progresses.

Girl's Names	Boy's Names

How big is my baby?

What changes are occurring in my baby?

How big am I?

How am I feeling?

How is my partner feeling?

Questions for my doctor

Things to do this week

Special thoughts and feelings about this week

A Place for Special Remembrances

Use this space for keeping
special mementoes in your journal.

Week 16

Take Good Care
of Your Teeth

*I*t's important to take good care of your teeth during pregnancy, just as it is when you're not pregnant. Throughout your pregnancy, practice good dental care—brush at least twice a day and floss at least once. Avoid foods that contain a lot of sugar. Drink lots of water to help keep teeth clean.

One good reason to continue to have regular dental checkups during pregnancy and to take good care of your teeth is that hormonal changes in pregnancy may cause dental problems. And if you experience nausea and vomiting, it's especially important to brush and floss regularly. Every time you vomit, your teeth come in contact with stomach acid, which can be very corrosive to your teeth.

During pregnancy, your gums may be more susceptible to irritation and may bleed more often when you brush your teeth. Your gums may be sore or swollen. You may develop small nodules on your gums that bleed when you brush your teeth or eat. These conditions usually clear up after pregnancy, but don't ignore them if they cause you problems. Talk to your dentist if *any* dental problem becomes uncomfortable or causes you worry.

You may have heard an old wives' tale about not going to the dentist during pregnancy. It's not true! Dental care during pregnancy is important for your good health.

If possible, avoid dental X-rays while you're pregnant. If you must have one, be sure your abdomen and pelvis are completely shielded by a lead apron. Tell your dentist you're pregnant when you check in at the office.

How big is my baby?

What changes are occurring in my baby?

How big am I?

How am I feeling?

How is my partner feeling?

Questions for my doctor

Things to do this week

Special thoughts and feelings about this week

Prenatal Classes

Prenatal classes are different from childbirth-preparation classes. These classes cover many aspects of pregnancy and can help you work more closely with your healthcare team during your pregnancy to help you enjoy this time. They can also help you prepare for your new baby. Many women take a series of classes that cover pregnancy in the early to middle part of their pregnancy. (Most women also take childbirth-preparation or childbirth-education classes, which prepare a woman to participate in the birth process. A chart for these classes is provided on page 109.)

Date of class	Time	Topics Covered

Week 17

Food Cravings—
They're Normal during Pregnancy

Are you craving some food that you don't normally eat? Do you sometimes feel you just *have* to eat a particular food or you'll burst?

It's normal to crave various foods during pregnancy. Many women do. (Sometimes the food you crave or when you crave it may seem very strange to other people!)

Food cravings can be good and bad for you. If you crave foods that are nutritious and good for you and baby, eat them in moderate amounts. If you crave foods that are high in sugar and fat, loaded with empty calories that offer little nutrition, be careful about eating them. Maybe a little taste will satisfy you. Sometimes it won't. You may have to exercise great restraint and will power *not* to eat a lot of something (which may happen with a food craving) that isn't beneficial for you.

We don't know why women crave unusual foods or food combinations during pregnancy. Hormonal and emotional changes that occur during pregnancy may have something to do with it. We've also found that some foods you normally love may make you sick to your stomach when you're pregnant. This is common. The hormones of pregnancy have a significant impact on the gastrointestinal tract, which can affect your reaction to certain foods.

You may have food cravings any time during pregnancy. Be cautious. If you eat everything you want, when you want it, you may lose control over your weight. When you crave a food that may not be the most nutritious, use self-control if you do indulge. You might try some other tricks, too. Substitute a low-fat food for a high-fat one, such as eating frozen yogurt instead of higher-calorie ice cream. You should be able to indulge in some of your cravings occasionally, if you do it wisely.

Do You Crave These Foods?

A recent study asked pregnant women what foods they craved and how much they craved them. The results were:

- Chocolate—33% of the time, women wanted chocolate
- Other sweets, desserts and ice cream—20% of the time, women craved these food items
- Citrus—19% of the time

If you crave any substances that are not good for you, talk with your doctor.

How big is my baby?

What changes are occurring in my baby?

How big am I?

How am I feeling?

How is my partner feeling?

Questions for my doctor

Things to do this week

Special thoughts and feelings about this week

A Place for Special Remembrances

Use this space for keeping
special mementoes in your journal.

Week 18

Ultrasound— It's the "Fun" Test

*M*any women have at least one ultrasound exam during their pregnancy. It may be one of the most exciting tests you have while you're pregnant! With this exam, you can actually see your growing baby moving inside you. Many doctors perform ultrasound exams on all of their pregnant patients, but not every doctor does. Some doctors perform ultrasounds only when there is a problem. You might want to ask your doctor at one of your early prenatal visits if you will have one during your pregnancy.

Ultrasound provides a 2-dimensional picture of the fetus. An instrument is placed on your abdomen or in your vagina to produce high-frequency sound waves that go through your skin and bounce off the baby. A computer then translates them into a picture. Some new ultrasounds provide a 3-dimensional picture. They are so clear that it looks like a photograph of the baby growing inside you!

There are many medical reasons for your doctor to do an ultrasound test. It can help determine your due date, discover how many babies you are carrying and tell your doctor other things about the developing fetus.

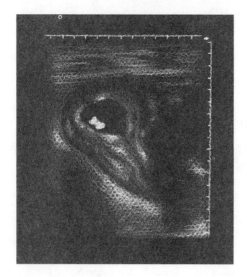

Ultrasound is an important test during pregnancy; it can tell your doctor many things.

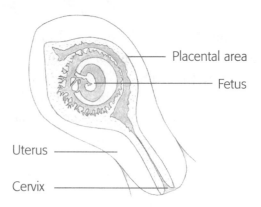

Placental area

Fetus

Uterus

Cervix

If you are at least 18 weeks pregnant (just about the point you are in pregnancy right now!) when you have your ultrasound, you *may* be able to determine the sex of your baby. But don't set your heart on it. It's not always possible to tell the baby's sex if its legs are crossed or it is in a breech position. Even if your doctor or the technician make a prediction about the baby's sex, remember an ultrasound is only a test, and tests can sometimes be wrong.

If You're Scheduled for an Ultrasound

If you are scheduled for an ultrasound exam, you might want to ask the following questions before you have the test.

- Can my partner or someone else (like my mother or mother-in-law) come to the test with me?
- Should we bring a blank videotape to record the ultrasound?
- Will we receive a picture or photograph of the baby taken during the test?

Use the space we have provided below to keep your baby's picture safe.

Ultrasound Photo

Date _____

Feelings and Thoughts _____

_____

How big is my baby?

What changes are occurring in my baby?

How big am I?

How am I feeling?

How is my partner feeling?

Questions for my doctor

Things to do this week

Special thoughts and feelings about this week

Week 19

When You Can't Wear Your Clothes, It's Time for a Maternity Wardrobe

*Y*ou may be excited about wearing maternity clothes. Most women want to show the world they are pregnant, and wearing maternity clothes is one way to do it. (If you're not especially excited, that's OK.)

You may not have to wear maternity clothes for a while. You may have some looser clothes that you can wear until it's more comfortable to buy "real" maternity clothes. You might be able to wear some of your partner's shirts, elastic-waist shorts or sweat pants (if they're not too enormous on you). A good rule of thumb is when you become uncomfortable wearing your regular clothes, it's time for maternity clothes.

When you shop for your clothing, choose natural fabrics when possible. Your metabolic rate may have increased, and you may feel warmer than usual. If you wear fabrics that "breathe," such as cotton in the summer and wool in the winter, you'll be more comfortable. You may also find layering your clothing in winter is helpful.

There are a lot of different styles of maternity clothes on the market today. See the box below for some ideas. Choose clothes that feel good to wear and that look good on you!

During your pregnancy, you'll discover lots of different maternity clothes that you might want to consider. Dresses, tops, pants and skirts are designed to allow you room to grow throughout your pregnancy. Undergarments that add support to your abdomen, breasts or legs are good choices. These include maternity bras, nursing bras, maternity panties and maternity support hose. You may even have to consider buying different shoes; swelling in your feet may cause an increase in your shoe size.

Some Popular Maternity-Clothes Styles

You may have a preference for the styles you choose, or you may have to shop to see what's available. Many women have found the following styles very comfortable to wear:

- Wide, elastic bands or panels that fit under your abdomen to provide support
- Wrap-around openings that tie and are easy to adjust
- Elastic waists that expand
- Button or pleated waistbands that are adjustable
- Waistbands that have slider to adjust fit

A helpful hint: If you want to wear your slacks or jeans a little while longer, "expand" the waist with a rubber band or an elastic loop. Looping one end over the button, place the rubber band through the buttonhole, and loop the other end over the button. Presto! You've added a few inches to the waistband of your pants.

How big is my baby?

What changes are occurring in my baby?

How big am I?

How am I feeling?

How is my partner feeling?

Questions for my doctor

Things to do this week

Special thoughts and feelings about this week

A Place for Special Remembrances

Use this space for keeping
special mementoes in your journal.

Week 20

You're halfway there!

It's Important to
Drink Lots of Fluid

*Y*our doctor may have suggested you drink extra fluid while you're pregnant. Extra fluid means drinking a *lot* of water every day!

Why is this important? Water helps the pregnant body process nutrients, develop new cells, sustain blood volume and regulate body temperature. Because your blood volume increases during pregnancy, drinking extra fluids helps you keep up with the change. You may also feel better during pregnancy if you drink more liquid than you normally do.

Drink at least six to eight 10-ounce glasses of liquid every day. Water is the best fluid; however, other fluids will satisfy your needs. Foods and drinks that can help you get enough fluid include juice, vegetables, milk and milk products, meats, grain products, fruits and some herbal teas. Avoid coffee, tea and diet cola when you can—they can contain sodium and caffeine, which act as diuretics.

Drinking a lot of fluid during your pregnancy can help you feel better in many ways.

Two quarts a day may seem like a lot to drink, but if you keep at it, you can do it. Some women drink one glass of water throughout the day. When it's empty, they refill it and drink on! (Decrease your intake later in the day so you don't have to get up to go to the bathroom all night long.)

If you suffer from headaches, uterine cramping and asthma, you may find increasing your fluid intake can relieve some symptoms. Drinking lots of water also helps avoid bladder infections and regulates body temperature, which is important if you have a fever.

Be aware that prenatal vitamins may make your urine a different color. It may appear more yellow than it normally does.

To see if you're drinking enough fluid, check your urine. When it's light yellow to clear, you're getting enough water. Dark-yellow urine is a sign that you need to increase your fluid intake.

How big is my baby?

What changes are occurring in my baby?

How big am I?

How am I feeling?

How is my partner feeling?

Questions for my doctor

Things to do this week

Special thoughts and feelings about this week

A Reminder: Around this time, you should be signing up for childbirth-education classes, which will begin in about 8 or 9 weeks. It's a good idea to sign up this far in advance to guarantee you will be able to get into the class you want to take.

Week 21

Feeling Baby Move—
What a Great Sensation!

About this time in your pregnancy, you should be feeling your baby move inside your uterus. It's one of the greatest joys of pregnancy and something a man can only be jealous of! (Feeling movement of the fetus is also called *quickening*.) Feeling your baby move can be very reassuring to you, and it is usually very enjoyable. Most women feel the baby move for the first time between 16 and 20 weeks.

You may feel your baby moving inside you for a few days before you realize what it is. Many women describe the first feelings of their baby's movement as a gas bubble or fluttering like a butterfly in their abdomen. As pregnancy progresses, movements become more common and frequent. At this point in your pregnancy, movement is felt below your bellybutton. (If it's your first baby, it is often 19 or 20 weeks before you are sure you feel the baby move.) As your pregnancy progresses, you'll feel baby moving everywhere! You might feel a foot kicking you in the ribs or a hand pressing on your pelvis. One woman described the sensation as "two cats in a sack fighting." Later she learned she was carrying twins!

As baby gets bigger, you'll be able to watch its movements! You'll be able to see the skin over your uterus moving when baby shifts position. Sometimes you can even see it through your clothes. Many parents-to-be enjoy sharing this experience and watch their baby's movements together. Encourage your partner to lay his hand on your tummy or lie next to you to allow him to feel the baby moving.

You probably won't feel your baby move every day at this point in pregnancy; that's normal. As your baby grows larger, movements become stronger and more regular. Between 20 and 32 weeks of pregnancy, the fetus can move between 200 and 500 times a day, kicking, rolling and wiggling!

Many women have said that when they felt their baby move, their pregnancy became more real and alive to them. It can be the beginning of your bonding with your baby.

How big is my baby?

What changes are occurring in my baby?

How big am I?

How am I feeling?

How is my partner feeling?

Questions for my doctor

Things to do this week

Special thoughts and feelings about this week

A Place for Special Remembrances

Use this space for keeping
special mementoes in your journal.

Week 22

Fish Is Good for You, and Baby, Too!

*E*ating fish during pregnancy is very healthful for you and your baby. Researchers have discovered the following important facts about eating fish and healthy pregnancies.

Fish contains omega-3 fatty acids, which may help prevent pregnancy-induced hypertension and pre-eclampsia. It may also enhance your baby's intellectual development.

Women who eat a variety of fish during pregnancy may have longer pregnancies and give birth to babies who weigh more. This is particularly important for baby.

It's a good plan to include fish in your diet—there are many to choose from. Most fish are low in fat and high in vitamin B, iron, zinc, selenium and copper. These are important nutrients during pregnancy.

Studies indicate that pregnant women should *not* eat some kinds of fish more than once a month. These fish include shark, swordfish and tuna (fresh or frozen). Other fish to avoid during pregnancy include some found in warm tropical waters, especially Florida, the Caribbean and Hawaii. Avoid the following "local" fish from those areas: amberjack, barracuda, bluefish, grouper, mahimahi, snapper and fresh tuna.

You may wonder if you should eat a particular fish. If you have questions, call the FDA's hotline; the number is listed below.

If you're unsure about whether you should eat a particular fish or if you would like further information, call the FDA on its toll-free telephone hotline: 800–332–4010.

Good Fish and Shellfish Choices

Eat these *fish* as often as you like: bass, catfish, cod, croaker, flounder, perch (freshwater and ocean), haddock, herring, mackerel, marlin, orange roughy, Pacific halibut, pollack, red snapper, salmon, scrod, sole.

Eat these *shellfish* as often as you'd like, if they are cooked thoroughly: clams, crab, lobster, oysters, scallops, shrimp.

How big is my baby?

What changes are occurring in my baby?

How big am I?

How am I feeling?

How is my partner feeling?

Questions for my doctor

Things to do this week

Special thoughts and feelings about this week

A Place for Special Remembrances

Use this space for keeping
special mementoes in your journal.

Week 23

"Can a Pickle Really Be Bad for Me?"
(Salt and Sodium Use during Pregnancy)

Has someone said to you during your pregnancy, "Be careful of the amount of salt you eat!"? They were warning you about more than salt—they were referring to *sodium,* which is contained in salt and a lot of other foods, too.

Sodium is a chemical that every body needs, to some extent, in the diet. This chemical maintains the proper amount of fluid in your body. (Table salt, a compound made up of sodium and chloride, is about half sodium.) During pregnancy, sodium can have an impact on you and also your baby. Using too much or too little of it can cause problems. You need some sodium; you just don't need a lot.

During pregnancy, it's a good idea to watch how much sodium you take in every day. Try to keep your intake of sodium under 3g (3000mg) a day. If you consume too much sodium, it can cause fluid retention, swelling and high-blood-pressure problems. For example, if you're watching your sodium intake and you eat a high-sodium food, such as a dill pickle, you may notice an increase in the swelling of your hands and feet the next day.

It's hard to avoid something unless you know where to find it. With sodium, that can be a problem. It's in your salt shaker and in salty-tasting foods, such as pretzels, potato chips, dill pickles and salted nuts. However, you can find it in foods that *don't* taste salty. Sodium is often used as a preservative in foods, such as canned and processed products; it can also be also found in large quantities in fast foods, cereals, desserts—even some medications.

How can you take control over consuming too much sodium? If sodium is a problem for you, shop for low-sodium or sodium-free foods. Read nutrition labels! You can also buy inexpensive pamphlets at larger grocery stores and bookstores that list the sodium content of common foods and fast foods.

Do You Use Too Much Salt?

Sometimes a person doesn't realize how much salt he or she uses. Try this experiment: Take the salt shaker off the table. Tell yourself and your partner that you won't use it for a week. Use salt in cooking, as you normally do, just don't add it to your food at the table. (Some people salt before they taste their food!) When the week is up, you may notice you don't need the extra salt, and you don't even miss it!

How big is my baby?

What changes are occurring in my baby?

How big am I?

How am I feeling?

How is my partner feeling?

Questions for my doctor

Things to do this week

Special thoughts and feelings about this week

A Place for Special Remembrances

Use this space for keeping
special mementoes in your journal.

Week 24

Sexual Intimacy during Pregnancy—It's How This All Started in the First Place!

*A*re you and your partner concerned about sexual intimacy during pregnancy? Is your partner more concerned with this aspect of your relationship? Are either of you afraid that having sex will hurt the baby in some way?

Your concerns are normal; most pregnant couples have these questions. Sex during pregnancy is an important topic; discuss it with your doctor. Bring up the subject at one of your prenatal visits, especially if your partner goes with you to your appointments. If he doesn't, assure him there should be no problems if your doctor gives you the go-ahead.

Your doctor's advice will be based on your particular pregnancy. Most doctors agree sex can be a part of a normal pregnancy. Neither intercourse nor orgasm should be a problem if you have a low-risk pregnancy. Frequent sexual activity should not be harmful to a healthy pregnancy either. Usually a couple can continue the level of sexual activity they are used to. A lot depends on how you feel. At least you don't have to worry about contraception.

Sexual intimacy is important to most couples. Pregnancy doesn't usually mean intimacy has to end during your pregnancy if you are a normal, healthy pregnant woman.

It may be reassuring to know that sexual activity doesn't harm a growing baby. The baby is well protected by the amniotic sac and amniotic fluid. Your uterine muscles are strong, which also help protect the baby. A thick mucus plug seals the cervix, which keeps infection out of the uterus.

Sex during pregnancy may be a different experience for you. In the first trimester, you may feel fatigued and nauseous. During the third trimester, your weight gain, growing abdomen, tender breasts and other changes may make you desire sex less. This is normal. Tell your partner how you feel, and try to work out a solution that works for both of you.

On the other hand, pregnancy may enhance your sex drive. In some cases, a woman experiences orgasms or multiple orgasms for the first time during pregnancy. This is due to heightened hormonal activity and increased blood flow to the pelvic area.

Some women feel less attractive during pregnancy because of their size and the changes in their bodies. Discuss your feelings with your partner. Some men find pregnant women very attractive. Tenderness and understanding can help you both.

Many couples say that the changes in the pregnant woman's body during pregnancy required some changes and adjustments in the couple's lovemaking, such as using different positions. These changes added some spice to their relationships, which opened the door to a little experimenting together that continued after the pregnancy.

How big is my baby?

What changes are occurring in my baby?

How big am I?

How am I feeling?

How is my partner feeling?

Questions for my doctor

Things to do this week

Special thoughts and feelings about this week

Week 25

Week beginning Sunday _____

Twins? Triplets? More?
"It Can't Be Happening to Me!"

*Y*ou and your partner may have recently learned you're expecting two or more babies; it may take a little time to recover from the surprise, if you've been planning on only one baby. You may be overwhelmed at the prospect of having two infants to care for. But once you recover, you may be overjoyed at the idea!

A multiple pregnancy occurs when a single egg divides after fertilization or when more than one egg is fertilized. Twins from one egg occur about once in every 250 births around the world. Twins from two eggs occur in 1 out of every 100 births in white women and 1 out of 79 births in black women. Hispanic women also have a higher incidence of twins. The occurrence of twins in Asian populations is less common—about 1 in every 150 births. Today, we are also seeing a rise in triplet births. However, a triplet birth is not very common; it happens about once in every 8000 deliveries.

If you're pregnant with more than one baby, take very good care of yourself. Extra rest is essential. You may need more than the recommended 2 hours of rest each day. Pay attention to what you eat; eat nutritiously. Plan to eat more food—you need at least 300 more calories *per baby* each day. Check with your doctor about exercising. You may be allowed to do some type of exercise, depending on your individual pregnancy.

When you are expecting more than one baby, your discomfort may be more pronounced, and it may begin earlier in pregnancy. You get "big" earlier, and you are larger than with a single pregnancy. This can cause some discomfort, so treat yourself well.

Take things more slowly during your pregnancy. Don't try to do too much. Let things go that are unimportant. Your house doesn't have to be spotless. You need to focus on your pregnancy so your growing babies get the best start in life that they can.

One woman who was carrying triplets and who hadn't taken fertility drugs came to an office visit wearing a T-shirt that read:

"Not one, not two, but three, and no drugs!"

She delivered three healthy girls; they went nicely with her three boys, ages 2, 5 and 8.

How big is my baby?

What changes are occurring in my baby?

How big am I?

How am I feeling?

How is my partner feeling?

Questions for my doctor

Things to do this week

Special thoughts and feelings about this week

A Place for Special Remembrances

Use this space for keeping
special mementoes in your journal.

Week 26

Pregnancy Involves You *and* Your Partner

*Y*our pregnancy is probably a very special time for you, but it may be a different experience for your baby's father. You may find your partner isn't excited about the maternity clothes you buy or the cute baby things you find at the store. A man is often somewhat removed emotionally from a pregnancy because he doesn't get to experience what it's like to have a baby growing inside him. All he can do is watch you.

Because your partner is less involved with the pregnancy than you are, don't expect the same level of interest and participation that you feel. You may have to adjust your expectations. You may need to encourage your partner to become more actively involved in your pregnancy. You can do this by asking him to go to your prenatal visits with you or by attending childbirth-education classes together. Sometimes a man needs to be directed on ways to help, and he may need to be told what he can do for you.

It's not unusual for a man to be a little jealous of the attention his pregnant partner receives. He may see the baby as a threat to his relationship with you. These are normal feelings.

Let your partner
be involved in the
pregnancy as
much as he wants
to be. Feeling
baby move is
enjoyable for both
of you.

Your partner can be a wonderful source of emotional support during your pregnancy, which can be important to both of you. Involve him as much as he is willing to be involved. Include him in important decisions about your pregnancy and the birth of your baby. Does he want to be your labor coach? Does he want to cut the umbilical cord? Or does he just want to hold your hand and not do much else? Let him decide what he wants to do and what he can or cannot do.

Some expectant fathers experience various physical problems during their partner's pregnancy. Don't be surprised if your partner has headaches, irritability, back and muscle aches, insomnia, fatigue or depression. Many of these symptoms are the body's way of signaling that tension is high and stress must be relieved. To do that, a father-to-be can talk with other men, such as those taking the same childbirth-education classes. When a man experiences stress-related symptoms during his partner's pregnancy, it's time for the couple to start taking better care of each other so together they can take care of their baby when it is born.

One Father-to-Be's
Personal "Pregnancy" Experience

A father-to-be recently agreed to don a "pregnancy belly" for an article in a women's magazine. He wore an apparatus that simulated the extra weight gained in the breasts, abdomen, hips and thighs of a pregnant woman. After wearing it for one day, he declared he understood why his wife was so tired and worn out. Lugging the extra 30 pounds was bad enough, but he was surprised by the activities it curtailed. One of his biggest difficulties? Leaning over and tying his shoes!

How big is my baby?

What changes are occurring in my baby?

How big am I?

How am I feeling?

How is my partner feeling?

Questions for my doctor

Things to do this week

Special thoughts and feelings about this week

Week 27

Do You Enjoy Tea Time?

*D*o you enjoy a cup of tea to warm you up or glass of tea to quench your thirst? In winter, a cup of hot tea can relax and calm you. In summer, a glass of iced tea can refresh you. Sitting down and drinking some tea can be a good time to reflect on your pregnancy and to write in your journal.

Because you're concerned about what you eat and drink, we have included some facts about regular teas and herbal teas to enlighten you about drinking tea during your pregnancy.

You don't have to be concerned about drinking regular tea during your pregnancy, if you drink it in moderation. Regular tea contains caffeine, so if you drink it later in the day, whether it's iced tea or hot tea, it might keep you awake. Tea can also act as a diuretic; if you drink a lot of it, you may urinate more or you might become slightly dehydrated. It makes sense to drink any tea in moderation.

Herbal teas are teas made from herbs not tea leaves. Many are commonly sold in grocery stores; others are harder to find and may need to be purchased at a health-food store. Many herbal teas are good for you and can help relieve certain pregnancy discomforts. This can make herbal tea a good alternative to coffee or regular tea. The herbal teas discussed below can relieve certain pregnancy problems and are delicious and safe to use during pregnancy.

Herbal teas to help you feel better include:

- chamomile—aids digestion
- dandelion—helps with swelling and can soothe an upset stomach
- ginger root—helps with nausea and nasal congestion
- nettle leaf—rich in calcium, iron and other vitamins and minerals
- peppermint—relieves gas pains and calms the stomach
- red raspberry—helps with nausea

Herbal Teas to Avoid during Pregnancy

Some herbs and herbal teas are *not* safe to use during pregnancy because they could harm your developing baby. Herbs and teas to *avoid* during pregnancy include:

Blue or black cohosh • pennyroyal leaf • yarrow • goldenseal • feverfew • psillium seed • mugwort • comfrey • coltsfoot • juniper • rue • tansy • cottonroot bark • sage (in large amounts) • senna • cascara sagrada • buckthorn • male fern • slippery elm • squaw vine

How big is my baby?

What changes are occurring in my baby?

How big am I?

How am I feeling?

How is my partner feeling?

Questions for my doctor

Things to do this week

Special thoughts and feelings about this week

A Place for Special Remembrances

Use this space for keeping special mementoes in your journal.

Week 28

Week beginning Sunday _____

It's Time to Start Your Childbirth-Education Classes

*Y*ou should be signed up for or ready to start your child-birth-education classes soon. Why so early? It's beneficial to start them now for a couple of reasons. One, it's a good idea to plan to finish the classes at least a few weeks before your due date. (Babies do come early sometimes!) Two, you'll have lots of time to practice various exercises and techniques with your labor coach, if you wish to use them during labor and delivery.

If your partner is going to act as your labor coach, a class can help you prepare for this very important event in your life! Nearly 90% of all first-time expectant parents take some type of childbirth-education class. If it's been a few years since you've had a baby, if you have questions or if you would like a review of labor and delivery, take a class. It's comforting to know that other pregnant couples have the same questions and concerns you have. Many of the things they ask about will be things you are wondering about or will want to know.

Classes are offered in various settings, such as a women's center, a birthing center or a childbirth association. Ask your doctor to recommend classes in your area. You might look in your yellow pages under "Childbirth Education." Most hospitals

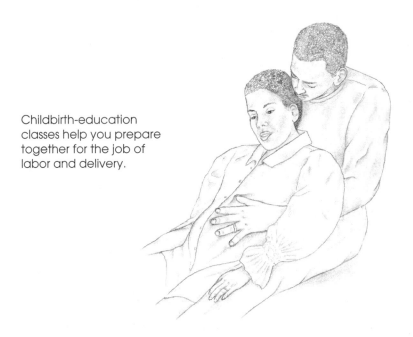

Childbirth-education
classes help you prepare
together for the job of
labor and delivery.

that deliver babies offer classes. They are often taught by labor-and-delivery nurses or a midwife.

You can benefit in many ways from taking a class. Studies show that women who take classes need less medication, have fewer forceps deliveries and feel more positive about the birth experience than women who do not take classes.

Classes cover many aspects of labor and delivery, including breathing techniques, vaginal birth, Cesarean delivery, hospital procedures, ways to deal with the discomfort and pain of labor and delivery, various pain-relief methods and the postpartum or recovery period. If you're expecting more than one baby, special classes may be offered.

Some insurance companies and a few HMOs offer partial or full reimbursement for class fees. Classes are usually reasonably priced.

Is a Childbirth-Education Class Right for You?

There may be several classes available in your area, but you're not sure which one will meet your particular needs. Here are some suggestions for evaluating a class:

• Find out what's available in your area.

• Talk to friends and relatives who have taken different classes.

• Decide whether you want a drug-free birth or whether you are willing to consider pain relief if it's necessary.

• Learn about the qualifications of the instructors in various programs.

• Visit some classes or talk to the teachers of a class in your area to choose the best one for you.

• Try to find classes that fit your partner's or your labor coach's schedule (if your partner will not be acting as your labor coach) so you can attend together.

How big is my baby?

What changes are occurring in my baby?

How big am I?

How am I feeling?

How is my partner feeling?

Questions for my doctor

Things to do this week

Special thoughts and feelings about this week

Childbirth-Education Classes

Childbirth-preparation classes can prepare you to work more closely with your healthcare providers during labor and delivery. Classes can help you and your labor coach begin working together as a team. They can also prepare you for life with your new baby. Most women take these classes with a partner to prepare them to participate in the childbirth process. Childbirth-preparation classes are usually taken from about the 30th week until just before you deliver.

Date of class	Time	Topics Covered

A Place for Special Remembrances

Use this space for keeping special mementoes in your journal.

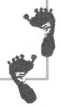

Week 29

Preparing Older Children
for Baby's Arrival

*I*f you have children already, you may be concerned about how to prepare them for the new baby. Begin by telling your children that a new baby will be joining the family. Then let them take it from there.

A friend had a T-shirt made for her 2 ½-year-old daughter to wear that stated: *"I'm going to be a Big Sister!"* It was very cute and a clever way to involve this little girl in the changes happening in her family.

When a child asks questions, give simple answers. For example, if your young child wants to know how the baby eats while it's growing inside you, an explanation such as "the baby gets its food from Mommy" will probably suffice. To your young child, your pregnancy isn't very important.

Wait to tell very young children about the baby until they can see for themselves it's growing inside you. Even then, it may be better to wait until you are fairly close to baby's birth to tell a very young child (under 3). When possible, use a familiar reference point for the birth, such as Christmas or when school gets out.

Older children may want more information. Answer their questions honestly, but even with older kids, don't provide more information than they need. With older children, ask your doctor if it's all right to bring one child at a time with you to a prenatal visit, so the child can listen to the baby's heartbeat. Or take your children to the hospital nursery to see the new babies. Many hospitals offer preparation classes for siblings; choose one suited to your child's age. You can also go to the library or bookstore to find books about pregnancy for children. There are some excellent books available, many with tasteful pictures and simple explanations.

Prepare children for your absence for the baby's birth. Let them know in advance who will care for them. When possible, include them in making this decision. It may be a good idea to have your children stay with someone they know and trust. If possible, allow your children to stay at home, where things are familiar. This is a time of great change for your older children, so try to make it as easy as possible on them. Jealousy, acting out and other behavioral changes are the norm.

Provide your children with extra love and attention during your pregnancy. Plan time alone together with each of them after your new baby is born.

How big is my baby?

What changes are occurring in my baby?

How big am I?

How am I feeling?

How is my partner feeling?

Questions for my doctor

Things to do this week

Special thoughts and feelings about this week

A Place for Special Remembrances

Use this space for keeping
special mementoes in your journal.

Week 30

Driving Safely during Pregnancy

*H*ave you ever been in a situation where you couldn't drive your car? You might have felt helpless or frustrated having to depend on others to go somewhere.

Driving a car is important to many women, but some wonder if driving during pregnancy is safe for them and their baby. In most normal pregnancies, it's usually safe to drive throughout pregnancy. You might find it gets difficult to fit comfortably behind the steering wheel and still keep your feet on the pedals as you get nearer to baby's birth. You might also have a harder time getting in and out of the car. But if you have no restrictions from your doctor, keep driving if you feel confident!

Ask your partner to help you if you need it. If you have two cars, you may find it is easier to drive one of them than it is to drive the other one. He can also adjust the seat and mirrors, and do other things that make it easier for you to drive. Trading parking places in the garage can even be beneficial. These situations may seem like a bother, but many couples look back fondly on these moments as memories of a time they grew closer together as a couple and as a family.

You may have questions or concerns about whether you should wear your seat belt and shoulder harness during pregnancy. For your protection, and the protection of your developing

Wear your seat belt
during your pregnancy;
it protects you and
baby while you're
riding in a car.

baby, *always wear your safety belt when driving or riding in a car!* These safety restraints are as necessary during pregnancy as they are when you're not pregnant! We have no evidence that use of safety restraints increases the chance of fetal or uterine injury. You have a better chance of surviving an accident wearing a seat belt than not wearing one.

There is a correct way to wear your safety belt during pregnancy. Place the lap-belt part of the restraint under your abdomen and across your upper thighs so it's snug but comfortable. Adjust your sitting position so the belt crosses your shoulder without cutting into your neck. Position the shoulder harness between your breasts; don't slip this belt off your shoulder. The lap belt cannot hold you safely by itself. If your car has a driver's side air bag, move your seat back so you have a little more room between your tummy and the steering wheel.

> Wearing a seat belt and shoulder harness are so important for a pregnant woman that the organization that uses crash test dummies to test cars has developed a pregnant dummy that includes a fetus. These devices help manufacturers create safer cars for everyone.

How big is my baby?

What changes are occurring in my baby?

How big am I?

How am I feeling?

How is my partner feeling?

Questions for my doctor

Things to do this week

Special thoughts and feelings about this week

A Place for Special Remembrances

Use this space for keeping
special mementoes in your journal.

Week 31

Don't Stop Now—Keep Taking Your Prenatal Vitamins

*S*ometimes later in pregnancy a woman stops taking her prenatal vitamins because she's tired of taking them or she decides they aren't necessary. It's important for you to take your prenatal vitamins every day for your *entire* pregnancy to ensure your good health and your baby's health. Many women continue taking their prenatal vitamins after baby's birth, especially if they are nursing. Ask your doctor about it. If your supply of vitamins is getting low and you believe you're close enough to delivery that you won't need to get a refill—get the refill and continue taking the vitamins even after delivery.

Prenatal vitamins contain the recommended daily amounts of vitamins and minerals you need throughout your pregnancy. You may wonder why you need to take a prenatal vitamin; isn't a multivitamin that you take when you're not pregnant just as good? The main difference is that prenatal vitamins contain extra iron and folic-acid supplements, which you need in larger amounts during pregnancy.

You may wonder if you need supplemental (extra) iron during pregnancy. The average woman's diet seldom contains enough iron to meet the increased demands of pregnancy. Your blood volume increases by 50% in a normal pregnancy. Iron is an important part of blood production in your body.

Prenatal vitamins contain some iron, but you may need to take extra iron. One of the first tests your doctor does is one for anemia. If he or she determines you need an iron supplement beyond the amount contained in your prenatal vitamins, it will be prescribed for you. Take it for your health and that of your baby.

In addition to taking your prenatal vitamins, eat nutritious, well-balanced meals to get the vitamins and minerals you and your baby need.

What's in Your Prenatal Vitamin?

You may want to know what's in your prenatal vitamin. Each vitamin contains many essential ingredients for the development of your baby and your continued good health. A typical prenatal vitamin contains the following:

- calcium to build baby's teeth and bones, and to help strengthen your own

- copper to help prevent anemia and to help in bone formation

- folic acid to reduce the risk of neural-tube defects and to help in red-cell production in the blood

- iodine to help control metabolism

- iron to prevent anemia and to help baby's blood development

- vitamin A for general health and body metabolism

- vitamin B_1 for general health and body metabolism

- vitamin B_2 for general health and body metabolism

- vitamin B_3 for general health and body metabolism

- vitamin B_6 for general health and body metabolism

- vitamin B_{12} to promote formation of blood

- vitamin C to aid in your body's absorption of iron

- vitamin D to strengthen baby's bones and teeth, and to help your body use phosphorus and calcium

- vitamin E for general health and body metabolism

- zinc to help balance fluids in your body and to aid nerve and muscle function

How big is my baby?

What changes are occurring in my baby?

How big am I?

How am I feeling?

How is my partner feeling?

Questions for my doctor

Things to do this week

Special thoughts and feelings about this week

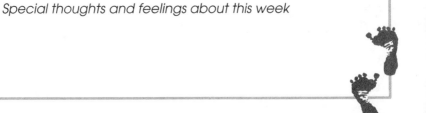

Week 32

Week beginning Sunday _____

Is It Hard to Get Enough Calcium in Your Diet?

Calcium is important in the diet of every pregnant woman. Your needs increase during pregnancy because your developing baby requires calcium to build strong bones and teeth, and you need calcium to keep your bones healthy.

During pregnancy, you need 1200mg of calcium a day. Most prenatal vitamins contain only a small amount of the calcium you need. If your calcium intake is inadequate, your baby may draw calcium from your bones.

Dairy products, such as cheese, milk and yogurt, are excellent sources of calcium and vitamin D, which is necessary for calcium absorption. You may also choose nondairy sources of calcium, such as legumes, spinach, some fish, nuts and other foods. Some common antacids are a good source of calcium. Read labels to learn if a food or substance contains calcium.

It's not uncommon to get tired of drinking milk or eating cheese or yogurt to get the calcium you need during pregnancy. Some suggestions that can add calcium to your diet are listed below.

Calcium is important for you and for baby. Drink milk, eat foods rich in calcium or take calcium supplements to be sure you get enough of this vital mineral.

- Make fruit shakes with milk and fresh fruit.
- Drink calcium-fortified orange juice.
- Add nonfat dried-milk powder to recipes.
- Cook brown rice or oatmeal in low-fat or nonfat milk instead of water.
- Drink calcium-fortified skim milk.
- Make soups and sauces with undiluted evaporated nonfat milk instead of cream.
- Eat calcium-fortified breads.

Some foods interfere with the body's absorption of calcium. Be careful about consuming salt, protein, tea, coffee and unleavened bread with a calcium-containing food.

How big is my baby?

What changes are occurring in my baby?

How big am I?

How am I feeling?

How is my partner feeling?

Questions for my doctor

Things to do this week

Special thoughts and feelings about this week

A Place for Special Remembrances

Use this space for keeping
special mementoes in your journal.

Week 33

Packing for the Hospital— Do It for Yourself!

*I*t's not too early to start thinking about packing for the hospital. You don't want to wait until the last minute, then throw your things together and take the chance of forgetting something important. If you don't get a chance to pack, your partner may do it for you. We've seen some strange things brought to the hospital by helpful partners; unfortunately a man's idea of what you need probably isn't yours! We've seen sexy lingerie, skimpy nightgowns and prepregnancy-sized jeans brought by "helpful" partners.

Start thinking now about what you want to take with you, then pack about 3 weeks before your due date. An advantage to beginning this task early is that you'll have time to think about what you really want to take with you. You'll avoid "panic packing," perhaps including items you don't need while forgetting more important ones. It also gives you time to wash and to prepare your selections or to buy other things you'll need, such as a nursing bra and nursing gowns. In addition to things you'll need, think about items to bring for your labor coach and items the baby will need after delivery.

Items to consider for your partner or labor coach for use during the birth include:

- a watch with a second hand
- talc or cornstarch for massaging you during labor
- a paint roller or tennis ball for giving you a low-back massage during labor
- tapes or CDs and a player, or a radio to play during labor
- camera and film
- list of telephone numbers and a long-distance calling card
- change for telephones and vending machines
- snacks for your partner or labor coach

The hospital will probably supply most of what you need for baby, but take a few things:

- clothes for the trip home, including an undershirt, sleeper, outer clothes (a hat if it's cold outside)
- a couple of baby blankets
- diapers, if your hospital doesn't supply them
- an approved infant car seat in which to take your baby home

Packing for Your Hospital Stay

There are a lot of things to consider, but the list below should cover nearly all of what you might need:

- completed insurance or preregistration forms and insurance card
- heavy socks to wear in the delivery room if your feet get cold
- an item to use as a focal point during labor
- 1 cotton nightgown or T-shirt for labor
- eyeglasses, if you wear them (you can't wear your contacts during labor)
- lip balm, lollipops or fruit drops to use during labor
- light diversion, such as books or magazines, to use during labor
- breath spray
- 1 or 2 nightgowns for after labor (bring a nursing gown if you are going to breastfeed)
- slippers with rubber soles
- 1 long robe for walking in the halls
- 2 bras (bring nursing bras and breast pads if you plan to breastfeed)
- 3 pairs of panties
- toiletries you use, including brush, comb, toothbrush, toothpaste, soap, shampoo, conditioner
- hairband or ponytail holder, if you have long hair
- loose-fitting clothes for going home
- sanitary pads, if the hospital doesn't supply them

How big is my baby?

What changes are occurring in my baby?

How big am I?

How am I feeling?

How is my partner feeling?

Questions for my doctor

Things to do this week

Special thoughts and feelings about this week

Week 34

Choosing Another Doctor—
This One for Baby

$\mathcal{I}$t's time to start thinking about choosing a doctor for your baby (usually a pediatrician). When possible, it's important to select and to visit the physician before your baby is born. Plan to visit the pediatrician about 3 or 4 weeks before your due date; if the baby comes early, you'll be prepared. When you register at the hospital or check in, they will ask you for the name of your pediatrician.

If you've never had a baby before, you may be unsure how to find a doctor for your baby. Ask your primary-care physician, your family practitioner, friends, co-workers and family members for names of pediatricians they know and trust. Or contact your local medical society and ask for a reference. If you belong to an HMO, and there is a group of physicians in pediatrics, arrange a meeting with one physician. If you have a conflict or don't see eye to eye with this person on important matters, you may be able to choose another pediatrician. Ask your patient advocate for information and advice.

The first visit is important; ask your partner to come with you. This is the time to ask questions about the care of your baby and to receive helpful suggestions. Discuss the doctor's

Meeting the doctor who will care for your baby is important for expectant parents.

philosophy, learn his or her schedule and "on-call" coverage, and clarify what you can expect of this physician. You can discuss circumcision for a baby boy, if you and your partner have questions or concerns.

When your baby is born, the pediatrician is notified and comes to the hospital to check the baby. In most instances, a pediatrician is not present at delivery unless there is a problem. A pediatric nurse from the nursery checks baby out immediately after birth and notifies the doctor. If everything is OK, the doctor visits baby the next morning, performs a physical on the baby and talks with you. Selecting a pediatrician before the birth ensures that your baby sees the same doctor for follow-up visits at the hospital and at the doctor's office.

After your visit, talk it over with your partner. Some issues can be resolved only by analyzing your feelings after the visit. If you decide you would rather choose a different doctor to care for your baby, you still have time to make another choice.

How big is my baby?

What changes are occurring in my baby?

How big am I?

How am I feeling?

How is my partner feeling?

Questions for my doctor

Things to do this week

Special thoughts and feelings about this week

A Place for Special Remembrances

Use this space for keeping
special mementoes in your journal.

Week 35

Preparing for Your Hospital Stay—
Do You Need a Reservation?

*Y*ou may want to do many things to prepare for your hospital stay before you actually go to the hospital to have your baby. Preregistering at the hospital a few weeks before your due date can be a time-saver when you go into labor, and it may help reduce your feelings of stress at that time.

You can preregister with forms you receive from your doctor's office or from the hospital. Fill out the forms early, even if . you don't submit them to the hospital before labor. If you wait until you're in labor, it may add to your stress. In addition to preregistering at the hospital, there are some other things you might want to do.

- Tour the labor and delivery area of your hospital.
- Talk to your doctor about what will happen during your labor.
- Find out who might cover for your doctor if he or she cannot be there for the birth.
- Plan the trip, and have your partner drive it a couple of times.

- Make alternative plans in case your partner can't be with you; have a back-up driver.
- If your partner isn't going to be your labor coach, plan how you will get in touch with your coach when you go into labor.
- Know how to get in touch with your partner 24 hours a day.
- Pack your bag with items for you, your labor coach or partner and the baby.

Everyone has heard amusing stories of babies delivered in a car, on a bus, in a taxi or on the way to the hospital. Fortunately, these things rarely happen. By planning ahead and being organized, you'll know that when your time comes, things should go smoothly.

How big is my baby?

What changes are occurring in my baby?

How big am I?

How am I feeling?

How is my partner feeling?

Questions for my doctor

Things to do this week

Special thoughts and feelings about this week

A Place for Special Remembrances

Use this space for keeping
special mementoes in your journal.

Week 36

Feeling Your Baby "Drop"

*O*ften a few weeks before labor begins or at the beginning of labor, your baby's head begins to enter the birth canal, and your uterus seems to "drop" a bit. This is called *lightening.* You may actually be able to see this change. Your uterus may be a little lower, and you may be able to breathe a little more easily.

A benefit of lightening is that you may be a little more comfortable sitting down because baby is not pressing so much on your upper body. However, as your baby descends into the birth canal, you may notice more pressure in your pelvis, bladder and rectum, which can be uncomfortable. You may have to go to the bathroom more often, or your hemorrhoids may be more uncomfortable. Take heart; it won't be long now till your baby is born!

How big is my baby?

What changes are occurring in my baby?

How big am I?

How am I feeling?

How is my partner feeling?

Questions for my doctor

Things to do this week

Special thoughts and feelings about this week

Do You Know When to Go to the Hospital?

You are probably concerned about when you should go to the hospital—that's natural. It's a subject to discuss at a prenatal visit.

There are three main symptoms that signal that baby's birth may occur soon. The list below is one to familiarize yourself with.

- Your water breaks.
- You are bleeding (more than just a little spotting).
- You have contractions that occur every 5 minutes and last 45 seconds to 1 minute.

Ask specifically whether you should call the doctor first or just go to the hospital if any of these symptoms occur.

Find out where you go. You may be directed to the emergency room or to labor and delivery.

Your baby may decide to come in the middle of the night (this often happens) or on a weekend. Your doctor will advise you of the best way to handle various situations.

A Place for Special Remembrances

Use this space for keeping
special mementoes in your journal.

Week 37

How Will You
Feed Your Baby?

*W*ill you breastfeed your baby? Will you bottlefeed him or her? It's something you may want to start thinking about, if you haven't already made a decision.

You may decide to breastfeed your baby; it's the best nutrition you can provide. In addition to your breast milk, baby also receives important nutrients, antibodies to help prevent infections and other substances important for his or her growth and development. You can usually begin breastfeeding your baby within an hour after birth. This provides baby with colostrum, which contains important factors that help boost the baby's resistance to infection.

You may choose to bottlefeed your baby; if you do, that's OK, too. You can still provide good nutrition for your baby. You just have to be aware of the various nutrients that different formulas provide. Ask your pediatrician for advice at your first visit (before baby's birth). The nurses in the hospital can also provide you with information.

You may not know what you want to do right now. You may still be trying to make up your mind. Some women know they want to try to breastfeed, no matter what. Others decide before

Breastfeeding baby provides the *best* nutrition for baby. But if you can't breastfeed, bottlefeeding also meets those nutritional needs.

baby's birth that they will bottlefeed. Either method can provide baby all the nutrition he or she needs to get a good start in life. There are advantages to both choices. If you haven't decided yet, you might want to talk with some friends about their experiences or discuss it at a prenatal visit. Either choice is a good one and requires your energy, attention and dedication.

Feeding is a great way to bond with your baby because of the closeness between you and baby that is created during the feeding process. If you breastfeed, you will bond with baby because of the physical contact of the baby nursing at your breast. If you bottlefeed, you can create this closeness by holding baby close and looking into his or her eyes. Talking and singing is a good way to establish closeness, no matter how you feed your baby. Dads can bond with baby by feeding him or her a bottle of expressed breast milk or a bottle of formula.

Feeding your baby is one of the most important tasks you will perform. The nutrition you give your baby will have an effect on the rest of his or her life.

How big is my baby?

What changes are occurring in my baby?

How big am I?

How am I feeling?

How is my partner feeling?

Questions for my doctor

Things to do this week

Special thoughts and feelings about this week

Baby Shower

Hostess _____

Date and time _____

Guests	Gifts

Baby Shower

Hostess _____

Date and time _____

Guests	Gifts

[photos]

[invitation]

Week 38

Will You Return to Work after Baby's Birth?

If you're like many women, after your baby is born, you will return to work. More than half of all mothers with pre-school-age children work outside the home. For almost all of them, finding adequate child care is a big issue.

If you're going back to work, it's not too early to start thinking about child-care arrangements. There is a shortage of child care for newborns and infants in the United States, so you may need to start planning *now* who will care for your baby when you return to work. This is especially important if you have more than one baby.

Arranging a child-care situation for your new baby can be one of the most important tasks you face before returning to work. The best way to choose the right setting and best care provider is to know your options. You do have choices. Any of a number of situations could be right for you; examine your needs and those of your child before you decide which to pursue. You may choose care in your home, care at another's home or care at a daycare center. Ask friends or family members what they do for childcare.

Babies have special needs; if you choose a daycare center, be sure it meets those needs. A baby must be changed and fed, but a baby needs to be held and interacted with, and comforted when he or she is afraid. A baby needs to rest at regular times each day. When searching for child care, keep in mind what is required for your child. Evaluate every situation in terms of how it meets your baby's needs.

To start the search for the right day care for your child, begin with the following ideas.

- Ask friends, family and co-workers for referrals to people or places they know about.
- Talk to people in your neighborhood.
- Ask at your church about programs they may sponsor.
- Call a local referral agency or contact Child Care Aware, 800-424-2246, for a local child-care resource.

No matter what kind of child-care situation you are considering, the best advice we can give you as parents who have been through the same experience is to check every situation out carefully and thoroughly before you make a final decision. Ask for references, and check them out. After you place your child in a situation, even if it's in-your-home care, drop in unannounced occasionally to see how things are going. **Trust your instincts!**

How big is my baby?

What changes are occurring in my baby?

How big am I?

How am I feeling?

How is my partner feeling?

Questions for my doctor

Things to do this week

Special thoughts and feelings about this week

A Place for Special Remembrances

Use this space for keeping
special mementoes in your journal.

Week 39

Get Ready for Baby—It's Too Late to Change Your Mind, Now!

You're probably getting pretty excited about meeting your baby and beginning your new life as a family. But you may have some questions about what you'll need when you bring baby home. You must decide what things you'll need to buy for baby. Then you need to shop for it all. Comparing prices can be a tedious task, but prices can vary a great deal, so it's probably worth it to comparison shop. You can easily spend over $7,500 the first year on baby's necessities and other basics (this includes setting up the nursery with crib, changing table and other items). When possible, borrow items from family and friends.

You may think all the baby does is eat and sleep, so why all the equipment, the clothes, the furniture? You may be surprised to discover all the things you will need and want for your baby.

Items to consider for the nursery include some sort of bed (crib, bassinet), a changing table, a chest of drawers, diaper pail, small lamp, mobile, vaporizer or humidifier and a smoke detector. Baby will also need some clothes to wear, although a newborn doesn't need too much. Diapers, T-shirts, gowns that open at the bottom, footed sleepers, socks, bibs, a hat, a warm

Of all the pieces of equipment you buy
for your baby, one of the most important
is an approved car seat. Be sure you
have one for baby's first ride home from
the hospital!

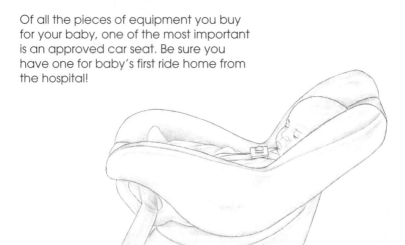

cover-up, one-piece short- or long-legged "onesies," blankets and towels are the most basic items to stock up on. How many of each you need depends on your personal situation, but it is recommended that you have about 8 dozen diapers on hand (order 100 a week for a newborn if you have a diaper service). This can be a combination of cloth and disposable diapers, if you choose. Both types are good in various situations.

In addition to clothes, you'll need some toiletries for baby. A brush and comb, nail clippers or scissors, nasal bulb syringe, an ear-type or rectal thermometer, baby shampoo, diaper-rash ointment, baby oil, baby powder, baby wipes, cotton balls and petroleum jelly can all come in handy when you need them. Buy some rubbing alcohol or pads soaked in rubbing alcohol (or make your own) to clean baby's umbilical-cord stump until it falls off. Keep items together so you'll be able to put your hands on them quickly.

A word of precaution: Be careful about buying second-hand nursery equipment or borrowing someone else's. Some items might not meet current safety standards.

How big is my baby?

What changes are occurring in my baby?

How big am I?

How am I feeling?

How is my partner feeling?

Questions for my doctor

Things to do this week

Special thoughts and feelings about this week

A Place for Special Remembrances

Use this space for keeping
special mementoes in your journal.

Week 40

Your Baby Is Due— Now What?

A few weeks ago, you may have thought that you would never make it to week 40. You may have been hoping that you would deliver early, and you would be home with your baby by now. However, only 5% of all pregnant women deliver on their actual due date; 90% deliver within a week of their baby's due date (either the week before or the week after). The others either delivered early or are considered overdue (their babies are born more than 2 weeks after their due date).

After all your anticipation, the prenatal visits you have made, the books and magazines you have read, the advice you have been given, the tests you have taken, the discomforts you've dealt with, the foods you have managed, the exercises you have done and the prenatal vitamins (and any other necessary medications) you have taken, you're almost there! Relax and take it easy. Your baby will be born when the time is right.

Waiting can create anxiety for you, but you have done a lot to prepare for this birth. Those taking care of you realize you may be anxious about what comes next. However, they are caring people who are experienced and skilled. They will care for you and your baby. Your partner and family and friends will also be there to support you.

You're ready! Allow yourself to enjoy the experience. You are part of a miraculous event that you may participate in only a few times in your life. Pat yourself on the back. You've done well.

It's time to meet your baby.

How big is my baby?

What changes are occurring in my baby?

How big am I?

How am I feeling?

How is my partner feeling?

Questions for my doctor

Things to do this week

Special thoughts and feelings about this week

A Place for Special Remembrances

Use this space for keeping
special mementoes in your journal.

After 40 Weeks

When Your Baby Is Late

*Y*our due date may have come and gone, and your baby is still not here. You may be getting very anxious to get your pregnancy over with. You may be wondering whether your doctor will induce your labor so your baby will be born. Is your baby overdue?

The definition of an overdue or *postterm baby* is one that is born 2 weeks or more past its due date. If your baby is overdue, it may be comforting to know most overdue pregnancies do well.

Doctors conduct tests on an overdue baby to determine its health and well-being inside the uterus. Labor is induced, when necessary. However, most doctors prefer not to induce labor; they would like you to go into labor naturally, and let labor and delivery happen on their own. It's OK to ask about induction, but understand that those taking care of you want what is best for you and your baby. Try not to pressure your doctor about induction.

Your doctor will do tests when he or she believes they are necessary. Your doctor can determine if the baby is moving around in the womb and if the amount of amniotic fluid is healthy and normal.

Even if your baby is overdue, he or she will be born soon. Birth is an incredible experience for both of baby's parents.

Tests that may be performed include a nonstress test, a contraction stress test and a biophysical profile. If problems are found, labor is often induced. If it is determined your baby is healthy and active, you are usually monitored until labor begins on its own.

It may be difficult to keep waiting for the big day to arrive, but try to relax and take it easy. Rest as much as you can. Take the extra time to prepare for the exciting day when you bring baby home.

How big is my baby?

What changes are occurring in my baby?

How big am I?

How am I feeling?

How is my partner feeling?

Questions for my doctor

Things to do this week

Special thoughts and feelings about this week

A Place for Special Remembrances

Use this space for keeping
special mementoes in your journal.

Appendix

Your Labor and Delivery

Hours of labor   Total weeks of pregnancy at delivery

Date of delivery   Time of delivery   am/pm

Place of delivery

Method of delivery   Vaginal   C-section

Complications of delivery

Name of person who delivered baby

People present at delivery

Special feelings at this important time

If I ever do this again, I would

Baby Facts

Baby's sex   Boy   Girl

(single   twin   more)

Birth weight   lbs.   oz.   Length   inches

Head circumference   centimeters

Apgar scores

Other tests done

Vitamin-K shot

Hepatitis vaccination

Chicken pox

Circumcision (for boys)   yes   no

Feeding problems or concerns

1st Meeting with Baby

Baby's first picture
(from hospital)

Bassinet card

ID Bracelet

What baby looks like

Now you're a family!

What baby smells like

What baby sounds like

Your Experience with Baby
In the Hospital

	For Mom	*For Dad*
Feelings		
Emotions		
What did you say?		
What did you do?		
First thought as a new parent		

Mom's After-Delivery Experience

First beverage

First meal

Special treats (that you've been waiting for!)

Flowers

Cards

Visitors

Phone calls

First time out of bed

Meeting with pediatrician

It's great to relax and to hold your baby close after all the long months of waiting. Enjoy being a mom!

Fun Facts—What's Going on in the World?

Weather on day of baby's birth

Headlines (save the entire newspaper
and put it in baby's keepsake box)

Sports events

Significant events

President of the United States

Price of gasoline

Baby's Health Going Home

Age at discharge   (hours, days, weeks)

Weight at discharge   lbs.   oz.

Jaundice   yes   no

Condition of umbilical-cord stump

Special instructions from doctor

First checkup appointment   Time   am/pm

Feeding instructions

Mom's 6-Week Checkup

Examined on

Name of doctor

Weight   lbs.   Gain or loss since last visit   lbs.

Blood pressure   /

Condition of episiotomy scar or C-section scar

Any postpartum problems or concerns

Questions you may have:

Is there anything I can do about sore breasts?

What are my birth-control options?

Can I begin an exercise program? When?

Is there anything I can do about postpartum blues?

What kind of vitamin supplementation should I take now?

When can we begin to have sexual intercourse again?

Is there anything from this pregnancy, labor and delivery I should know about for the next pregnancy?

When can I try to get pregnant again?

Medical History and Prenatal Visits

My Health History

Age   Date of birth

Hospital and city of birth

Height   ft.   in.

Prepregnancy weight   lbs.

Anticipated weight gain   lbs.

Blood type   Rh factor   Rubella titer

Last menstrual period (LMP)   Last Pap smear

My Health History

Estimated date of delivery (EDC)

Name of baby's father

Health problems (previous, current or chronic)

Surgeries

Allergies

Name(s) of doctor(s)

My Medication History

List medications you were taking when you got pregnant and those you currently take. Include all over-the-counter (non-prescription medications) and any vitamins, minerals or herbs you take.

Medication	Date Started	Date Stopped	Reason for Use

My Pregnancy History

Date of birth	Sex	Delivered at how many weeks?	Birth weight	*Special notes about delivery or C-section

---

*Include number of hours in labor, anesthesia, type of delivery, number of weeks pregnant, complications.

1st Prenatal Visit 🖊

Date

Examined on   when I was   weeks pregnant.

Name of doctor

Baby's due date

(Check if done during this visit; record results and other information below.)

Weight   lbs.   Gain since becoming pregnant   lbs.

Blood pressure   /

Lab tests

Problems or concerns

Questions you may want to ask:

What types of food should I eat?

How much weight should I gain?

Do I need to take prenatal vitamins?

Do I need to take iron?

What is normal blood pressure for me?

How long will I have morning sickness?

What can I do about morning sickness?

Can the baby's father come with me to my prenatal visits?

What can I do to increase my energy when I'm feeling fatigued or tired?

Will I have to have any special tests, such as amniocentesis, alpha-fetoprotein, ultrasound?

2nd Prenatal Visit

Date

Examined on   when I was   weeks pregnant.

Name of doctor

Baby's due date

(Check if done during this visit; record results and other information below.)

Weight   lbs.   Gain since becoming pregnant   lbs.

Blood pressure   /

Lab tests

Baby's heartbeat checked

Other

Problems or concerns

Questions you may want to ask:

How much can I safely exercise?

What kinds of exercise are safe for me?

Can I still have sexual intercourse?

What were the results of my lab tests?

Is it important to get dental care while I'm pregnant?

How am I doing with my weight?

Should I perform a breast self-examination?

How does my age affect my pregnancy?

3rd Prenatal Visit 🖊

Date

Examined on   when I was   weeks pregnant.

Name of doctor

Baby's due date

(Check if done during this visit; record results and other information below.)

Weight   lbs.   Gain since becoming pregnant   lbs.

Blood pressure   /

Lab tests

Baby's heartbeat checked

Other

Problems or concerns

Questions you may want to ask:

What can I do to relieve backaches?

Why is anemia so common during pregnancy?

Will I be having an ultrasound?

When will I feel my baby move?

What is an AFP test?

Do I need an AFP test?

What will it tell me about my baby?

4th Prenatal Visit

Date

Examined on   when I was   weeks pregnant.

Name of doctor

Baby's due date

(Check if done during this visit; record results and other information below.)

Weight   lbs.   Gain since becoming pregnant   lbs.

Blood pressure   /

Lab tests

Baby's heartbeat checked

Other

Problems or concerns

Questions you may want to ask:

What prenatal classes are available?

When do classes start?

Why am I short of breath?

What can I do about it?

What are the advantages of breastfeeding my baby?

Are there any advantages to bottlefeeding my baby?

What is the danger to me if I change my cat's litter box?

5th Prenatal Visit

Date

Examined on   when I was   weeks pregnant.

Name of doctor

Baby's due date

(Check if done during this visit; record results and other information below.)

Weight   lbs.   Gain since becoming pregnant   lbs.

Blood pressure   /

Lab tests

Baby's heartbeat checked

Abdomen measured (centimeters)

Other

Problems or concerns

Questions you may want to ask:

What is RhoGAM?

If I'm Rh negative, why do I need an injection of RhoGAM?

What can I do to prevent or lessen my chances of developing varicose veins?

What causes skin blotches?

How long will I have these skin blotches?

Should I be taking it easier at work?

6th Prenatal Visit

Date

Examined on   when I was   weeks pregnant.

Name of doctor

Baby's due date

(Check if done during this visit; record results and other information below.)

Weight   lbs.   Gain since becoming pregnant   lbs.

Blood pressure   /

Lab tests

Baby's heartbeat checked

Abdomen measured (centimeters)

Other

Problems or concerns

Questions you may want to ask:

What are Braxton-Hicks' contractions?

What can I do to relieve the discomfort of hemorrhoids?

What can I do to relieve the discomfort of constipation?

Can I still exercise?

What kinds of exercise should I be doing?

What is gestational diabetes?

How will I know if I have it?

7th Prenatal Visit

Date

Examined on   when I was   weeks pregnant.

Name of doctor

Baby's due date

(Check if done during this visit; recordresults and other information below.)

Weight   lbs.   Gain since becoming pregnant   lbs.

Blood pressure   /

Lab tests

Baby's heartbeat checked

Abdomen measured (centimeters)

Other

Problems or concerns

Questions you may want to ask:

What effects can anemia have on my pregnancy?

What should I do about swelling in my hands and feet?

Can I do anything to decrease stretch marks?

Can I still have sexual intercourse?

8th Prenatal Visit

Date

Examined on   when I was   weeks pregnant.

Name of doctor

Baby's due date

(Check if done during this visit; record results and other information below.)

Weight   lbs.   Gain since becoming pregnant   lbs.

Blood pressure   /

Lab tests

Baby's heartbeat checked

Abdomen measured (centimeters)

Other

Problems or concerns

Questions you may want to ask:

When should I get concerned if I don't feel my baby move?

What can I do to increase my energy when I'm feeling tired and fatigued?

Why is breathing easier for me now than it was earlier?

Is it OK to go swimming at this time?

Who can I have with me during labor and delivery?

What types of pain relief are available to me during labor and delivery?

How will they affect my baby?

How can I tell if I'm really in labor?

9th Prenatal Visit

Date

Examined on   when I was   weeks pregnant.

Name of doctor

Baby's due date

(Check if done during this visit; record results and other information below.)

Weight   lbs.   Gain since becoming pregnant   lbs.

Blood pressure   /

Lab tests

Baby's heartbeat checked

Abdomen measured (centimeters)

Other

Problems or concerns

Questions and Notes about Birth Options*

_____

_____

_____

_____

_____

_____

_____

_____

_____

_____

_____

_____

_____

_____

_____

*Birth options may include pain medication, positions in labor and delivery, walking early in labor, intermittent or constant fetal heart monitoring, length of hospital stay, rooming in.

10th Prenatal Visit

Date

Examined on   when I was   weeks pregnant.

Name of doctor

Baby's due date

(Check if done during this visit; record results and other information below.)

Weight   lbs.   Gain since becoming pregnant   lbs.

Blood pressure   /

Lab tests

Baby's heartbeat checked

Abdomen measured (centimeters)

Other

Problems or concerns

Questions you may want to ask:

What is a forceps delivery? Why is it sometimes necessary?

Can I nurse my baby immediately after I deliver?

What is "bonding"?

Will the birthing facility allow "rooming in" with my baby?

Why do some people have their babies by Cesarean section (C-section)?

What can I expect if I must deliver by Cesarean section (C-section)?

11th Prenatal Visit

Date

Examined on   when I was   weeks pregnant.

Name of doctor

Baby's due date

(Check if done during this visit; record results and other information below.)

Weight   lbs.   Gain since becoming pregnant   lbs.

Blood pressure   /

Lab tests

Baby's heartbeat checked

Abdomen measured (centimeters)

Other

Problems or concerns

Questions you may want to ask:

How many people can I have in the labor and delivery room with me?

Do they have to be family, or can others come in too?

Is it OK to take pictures of the delivery or other activities in the delivery room?

Can we videotape the delivery?

Will you be at the hospital when I get there in labor?

Are there any situations in which I won't be able to have someone with me when I deliver, such as if I have to have a Cesarean section?

12th Prenatal Visit

Date

Examined on   when I was   weeks pregnant.

Name of doctor

Baby's due date

(Check if done during this visit; record results and other information below.)

Weight   lbs.   Gain since becoming pregnant   lbs.

Blood pressure   /

Lab tests

Baby's heartbeat checked

Abdomen measured (centimeters)

Other

Problems or concerns

Questions you may want to ask:

Have I started to dilate yet?

How will I know when my membranes rupture?

When should I call my doctor?

When should I go to the hospital?

Can someone be with me if I have a C-section?

Can I breastfeed my baby if I have a C-section?

13th Prenatal Visit 🖊

Date

Examined on   when I was   weeks pregnant.

Name of doctor

Baby's due date

(Check if done during this visit; record results and other information below.)

Weight   lbs.   Gain since becoming pregnant   lbs.

Blood pressure   /

Lab tests

Baby's heartbeat checked

Abdomen measured (centimeters)

Other

Problems or concerns

Questions you may want to ask:

When I think I am in labor, whom should I call?

Should I just go to the hospital?

14th Prenatal Visit

Date

Examined on   when I was   weeks pregnant.

Name of doctor

Baby's due date

(Check if done during this visit; record results and other information below.)

Weight   lbs.   Gain since becoming pregnant   lbs.

Blood pressure   /

Lab tests

Baby's heartbeat checked

Abdomen measured (centimeters)

Other

Problems or concerns

Questions you may want to ask:

If I go past my due date, what happens?

Is it OK for the baby if I go over 40 weeks?

What does it mean to be "induced"?

Also by Glade B. Curtis, M.D. and Judith Schuler, M.S.

Your Pregnancy Week by Week
Your Pregnancy Questions and Answers
Your Pregnancy—Every Woman's Guide
Your Pregnancy After 35
Your Baby's First Year, Week by Week
Bouncing Back After Your Pregnancy